"You are as welcome as the flowers in May."

Charles Macklin

First published 1997
This edition © Robert Frederick Ltd. 2000
4, North Parade Buildings, Bath BA1 1LF, England

Editorial selections © Robert Frederick Ltd. All rights reserved.

Printed and bound in India.

Guest Book

messages from our guests and visitors
illustrated in colour

Guest Book

"The ornament of a house is the friends who frequent it."

Ralph Waldo Emerson

Name & Address   *Date*

Comments

Name & Address   *Date*

Comments

Name & Address   *Date*

Comments

Name & Address   *Date*

Comments

Name & Address   *Date*

Comments

the masterpiece of friendship

"All love is sweet,
Given or returned.   Common as light is love,
And its familiar voice wearies not ever."

Shelley

Name & Address

Date

Comments

Name & Address

Date

Comments

Name & Address

Date

Comments

Guest Book

Name & Address

Date

Comments

Name & Address

Date

Comments

Name & Address

Date

Comments

Name & Address

Date

Comments

Guest Book

Name & Address

Date

Comments

Name & Address

Date

Comments

Name & Address

Date

Comments

Name & Address

Date

Comments

Guest Book

Name & Address

Date

Comments

Name & Address

Date

Comments

Name & Address

Date

Comments

Name & Address

Date

Comments

*"The most wasted day is that in which
we have not laughed."*

Chamfort

Guest Book

Name & Address   Date

Comments

Name & Address   Date

Comments

Name & Address   Date

Comments

Name & Address   Date

Comments

Name & Address   Date

Comments

Name & Address   Date

Comments

Guest Book

Name & Address   Date

Comments

Name & Address   Date

Comments

Name & Address   Date

Comments

Name & Address   Date

Comments

Name & Address   Date

Comments

Name & Address   Date

Comments

Guest Book

Name & Address   *Date*

Comments

"We only part to meet again."
John Gay

Name & Address   *Date*

Comments

Guest Book

❦

Name & Address   Date

Comments

Name & Address   Date

Comments

Name & Address   Date

Comments

Name & Address   Date

Comments

"All other things to their destruction draw,
Only our love hath no decay;
This, no tomorrow hath, nor yesterday,
Running it never runs from us away,
But truly keeps his first, last, everlasting day."

John Donne

first, last, everlasting day

Guest Book

Name & Address   Date

Comments

Name & Address   Date

Comments

Name & Address   Date

Comments

Name & Address   Date

Comments

Name & Address   Date

Comments

Name & Address   Date

Comments

Guest Book

Name & Address   Date

Comments

Name & Address   Date

Comments

Name & Address   Date

Comments

Name & Address   Date

Comments

Name & Address   Date

Comments

Name & Address   Date

Comments

Guest Book

Name & Address   Date

Comments

Name & Address   Date

Comments

Name & Address   Date

Comments

"To the art of working well a civilised race would add the art of playing well."

Ralph Waldo Emerson

Guest Book

Name & Address   Date

Comments

Name & Address   Date

Comments

Name & Address   Date

Comments

Name & Address   Date

Comments

"The home of everyone is to him his castle and fortress,
as well for his defence against injury and violence, as for his repose."
Edward Coke

Name & Address   Date

Comments

Guest Book

Name & Address

Comments

Name & Address

Comments

Name & Address

Comments

Name & Address

Comments

Name & Address

Comments

"The joys of meeting
pay the pangs of absence;
Else who could bear it?"
Nicholas Rowe

Guest Book

Name & Address

Date

Comments

"When there is room in the heart there is room in the house."
Danish Proverb

Guest Book

Name & Address   Date

Comments

Name & Address   Date

Comments

Name & Address   Date

Comments

Name & Address   Date

Comments

"The return makes one love the farewell."
Alfred de Musset

Name & Address   Date

Comments

Guest Book

Name & Address

Date

Comments

Name & Address

Date

Comments

Name & Address

Date

Comments

*"Good company and good discourse
are the very sinews of virtue."*
Izaak Walton

Guest Book

Name & Address   Date

Comments

Name & Address   Date

Comments

Name & Address   Date

Comments

Name & Address   Date

Comments

Name & Address   Date

Comments

Name & Address   Date

Comments

Guest Book

❦

Name & Address   Date

Comments

Name & Address   Date

Comments

"God gave us memories that we might have roses in December."

James M. Barrie

Name & Address   Date

Comments

Guest Book

Name & Address

Date

Comments

Name & Address

Date

Comments

Name & Address

Date

Comments

Name & Address

Date

Comments

"*Love, all alike, no season knows, nor clime,*
Nor hours, age, months, which are the rags of time."

John Donne

Guest Book

Name & Address

Date

Comments

Name & Address

Date

Comments

Name & Address

Date

Comments

Name & Address

Date

Comments

the wing of friendship

"What is the odds so long as
the fire of soul is kindled at
the taper of conviviality,
and the wing of friendship never
moults a feather?"

*Charles Dickens:
The Old Curiosity Shop*

"A friend is a gift you give yourself."
Robert Louis Stevenson

Guest Book

Name & Address

Date

Comments

Name & Address

Date

Comments

Name & Address

Date

Comments

Name & Address

Date

Comments

Name & Address

Date

Comments

Name & Address

Date

Comments

Guest Book

Name & Address   *Date*

Comments

Name & Address   *Date*

Comments

Name & Address   *Date*

Comments

the masterpiece of nature

Name & Address   *Date*

Comments

"*A friend may
well be reckoned
the masterpiece
of nature.*"

Ralph Waldo Emerson

Guest Book

Name & Address

Comments

Date

Name & Address

Comments

Date

Name & Address

Comments

Date

Guest Book

Name & Address

Date

Comments

Name & Address

Date

Comments

Name & Address

Date

Comments

Name & Address

Date

Comments

Name & Address

Date

Comments

Guest Book

Name & Address

Comments

Date

Name & Address

Comments

Date

Name & Address

Comments

Date

Name & Address

Comments

Date

Name & Address

Comments

Date

Name & Address

Comments

Date

Guest Book

Name & Address

Date

Comments

Name & Address

Date

Comments

Name & Address

Date

Comments

Name & Address

Date

Comments

"What is this life if, full of care,
We have no time to stand and stare."

W. H. Davies

Guest Book

"Strange to see how a good dinner and feasting reconciles everybody."

Samuel Pepys

Name & Address   *Date*

Comments

Name & Address   *Date*

Comments

Name & Address   *Date*

Comments

Guest Book

Name & Address

Comments

Name & Address

Comments

Name & Address

Comments

Name & Address

Comments

Name & Address

Comments

Name & Address

Comments

Date

Date

Date

Date

Date

Date

Guest Book

Name & Address   Date

Comments

"Happiness makes up in height for what it lacks in length."

Robert Frost

Name & Address   Date

Comments

G. Van Spaendo

Guest Book

Name & Address

Date

Comments

Name & Address

Date

Comments

Name & Address

Date

Comments

Name & Address

Date

Comments

Guest Book

Name & Address

Date

Comments

Name & Address

Date

Comments

Name & Address

Date

Comments

Name & Address

Date

Comments

Guest Book

❦

Name & Address

Date

Comments

Name & Address

Date

Comments

Name & Address

Date

Comments

Name & Address

Date

Comments

"There is no hope of joy except in human relations."
Saint-Exupéry

Guest Book

Name & Address   Date

Comments

Name & Address   Date

Comments

Name & Address   Date

Comments

Name & Address   Date

Comments

Name & Address   Date

Comments

Name & Address   Date

Comments

Guest Book

Name & Address   Date

Comments

Name & Address   Date

Comments

Name & Address   Date

Comments

Name & Address   Date

Comments

Name & Address   Date

Comments

Name & Address   Date

Comments

greet as angels greet

Though seas and land
betwixt us both
Our faith and troth,
Like separated souls,
All time and space controls:
Above the highest sphere we meet,
Unseen, unknown;
and greet as angels greet.

Richard Lovelace

Guest Book

Name & Address   Date

Comments

Name & Address   Date

Comments

Name & Address   Date

Comments

Name & Address   Date

Comments

Name & Address   Date

Comments

"Bliss in possession will not last;
Remembered joys are never past."

James Montgomery

Guest Book

Name & Address   Date

Comments

Name & Address   Date

Comments

Name & Address   Date

Comments

Name & Address   Date

Comments

Name & Address   Date

Comments

Name & Address   Date

Comments

Guest Book

Name & Address

Date

Comments

as welcome as the flowers

"*You are as welcome as
the flowers in May.*"
Charles Macklin

Guest Book

"There's nothing worth the wear of winning,
But laughter and the love of friends."

Hilaire Belloc

Name & Address   Date

Comments

Name & Address   Date

Comments

Name & Address   Date

Comments

Name & Address   Date

Comments

Name & Address   Date

Comments

Acknowledgements

A Still Life of Roses by F. Fenetti (19th/20th Century), Sotheby's Picture Library; A Still Life of Roses in a Vase by Paul Biva (1851-1900), Sotheby's Picture Library; The Empress Comes (or "Poppea Comes") by George Lawrence (1858-1933), Sotheby's Picture Library; Sunflowers by Claude Monet (1840-1926); The Artist's Garden, Irises by Claude Monet (1840-1926); The Luncheon by Claude Monet (1840-1926); Fresh from the Altar by Jessica Hayllar (1858-1940), Christie's, London/Bridgeman Art Library, London; A Still Life of Peonies in a Vase by Marguerite Carrier-Roy, (B1870), Sotheby's Picture Library; At the Piano by Auguste Renoir (1841-1919); Villa at Reuil by Edouard Manet (1832-1888); The Garden of Les Mathurins at Pontoise by Camille Pissarro (1830-1903); Houses at Argenteuil by Claude Monet (1840-1926); The Luncheon of the Boating Party by Auguste Renoir (1841-1919); A Still Life of Roses by F. Fenetti (19th/20th Century), Sotheby's Picture Library; At Cocking, Sussex by James Matthews, Harper Fine Art, Fine Art Photograph Library; Anne Hathaway's Cottage by Arthur Claude Strachan (1865-1954), Haynes Fine Art, Fine Art Photograph Library; Roses on a Riverbank by Madeleine Lemaire (1845-1928), Sotheby's Picture Library; Women in the Garden by Claude Monet (1840-1926); A Still Life of Roses by F. Fenetti (19th/20th Century), Sotheby's Picture Library; Fruit, Still Life by Jan Van Huysum (1682-1749); The Year's at Spring, All's Right with the World by Sir Lawrence Alma-Tadema (1836-1912), Sotheby's Picture Library; Still Life, 1651 by Willem Claesz Heda; The Red Roofs, Corner of a Village, Winter by Camille Pissarro (1830-1903); A Still Life of Grapes Resting on a Marble Ledge by G. Van Spaendonck (1746-1822), Rafael Valls Gallery, London/Bridgeman Art Library, London; Garden at Argenteuil by Claude Monet (1840-1926); The Swing by Auguste Renoir (1841-1919); The Shrine by John William Waterhouse (1849-1917), Christopher Wood Gallery, London/Bridgeman Art Library, London; Poppies at Argenteuil by Claude Monet (1840-1926); The Soul of the Rose by John William Waterhouse (1849-1917), Christie's Photo Library, London ; Under the Arbour at the Moulin de la Galette by Auguste Renoir (1841-1919)
Other images © Robert Frederick Ltd. 1997